THE HOSPITAL

David and Patricia Armentrout

Rourke
Publishing LLC
Vero Beach, Florida 32964

www.rourkepublishing.com

PHOTO CREDITS: © Francis Twitty: cover; © Melissa Carroll: page 5; © Frances Twitty: page 6; © Yvonne Chamberlain: page 8; © Rick Rhay: page 9; © Jim Parkin: page 10; © Paolo Florendo: page 11; © Tomaz Levstek: page 15; © Roberta Osborne: page 17; © Rarpia: page 18; © Blaney Photo: page 19; © Sean Locke: page 20; © Talk Kienas: page 21; © Milan Radulovic: page 22

Edited by Kelli Hicks

Cover design by Teri Intzegian
Interior design by Teri Intzegian

Library of Congress Cataloging-in-Publication Data

Armentrout, David, 1962-
  The hospital : our community / David and Patricia Armentrout.
     p. cm. -- (Our community)
  ISBN 978-1-60472-337-3
  1. Hospitals--Juvenile literature. I. Armentrout, Patricia, 1960- II. Title.
  RA963.5.A76 2009
  362.11--dc22
                              2008016344

Printed in the USA

CG/CG

Rourke Publishing

www.rourkepublishing.com – rourke@rourkepublishing.com
Post Office Box 3328, Vero Beach, FL 32964

Table of Contents

A Hospital Nearby

Sometimes people get sick or hurt. When medical care at home can't solve the problem, it's comforting to know a hospital is nearby.

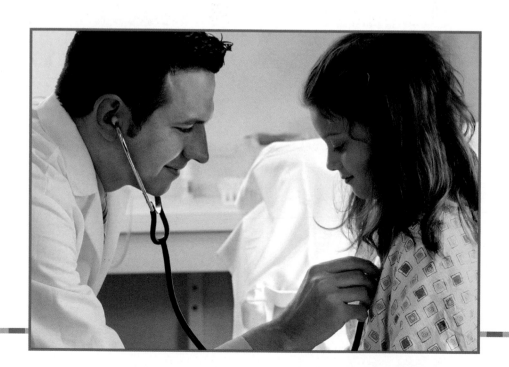

Do you have a hospital in your community?

A hospital is a place people go for **expert** medical care. Communities depend on hospitals and the trained workers that are on duty to help.

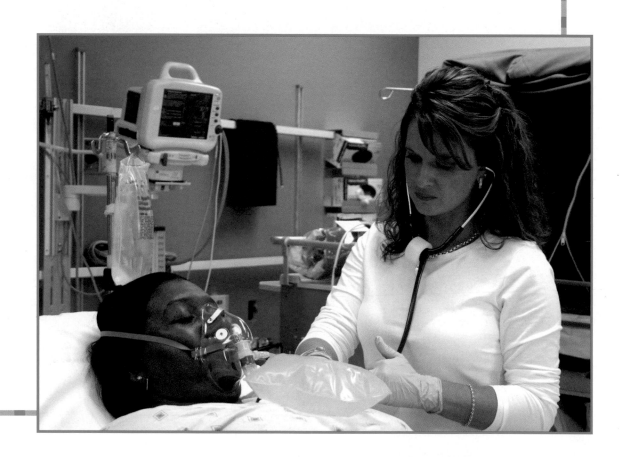

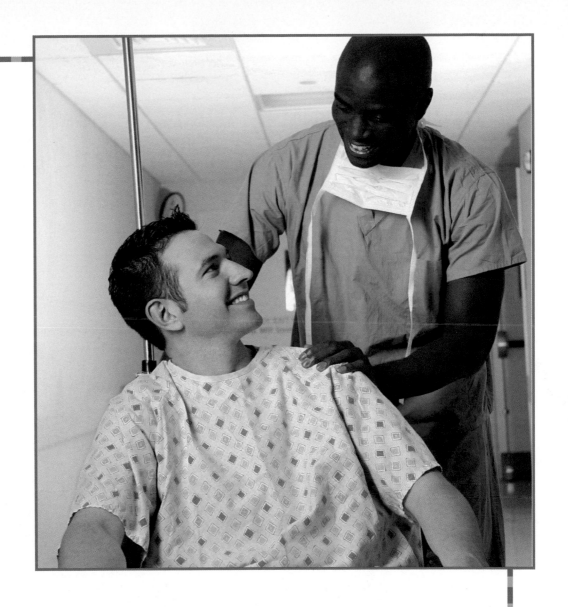

Hospitals provide medical care 24 hours a day.

Hospitals are filled with patients, their family and friends, and of course, doctors and nurses.

A nurse checks a patient's blood pressure.

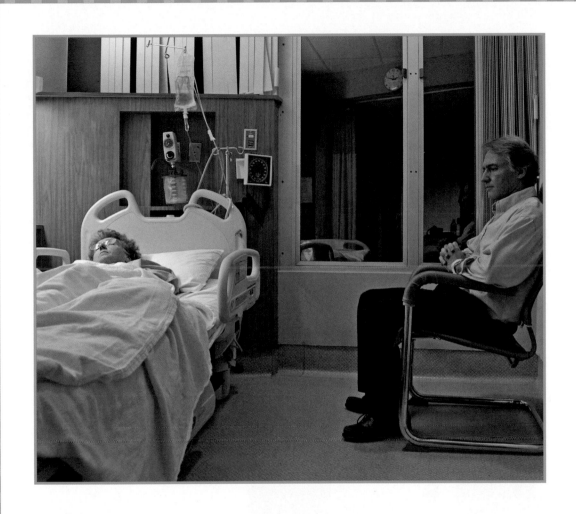

Patients appreciate visits
from family members.

Large hospitals have several buildings with many floors. Finding your way can be confusing.

Signs at the hospital entrance point visitors to the right building.

→ **Labor & Delivery**

→ **401 - 429**

→ **Maternity Waiting**

→ **Nursery**

→ **Obstetric Center**

→ **Post Partum**

→ **Sleep Disorders Ctr.**

← **Outpatient Care Ctr.**

← **430 - 443**

Hallway signs help people locate different hospital departments.

Emergency Care

The emergency department is for patients who need immediate or urgent medical care. Injuries like cuts, burns, and broken bones bring people to the emergency room.

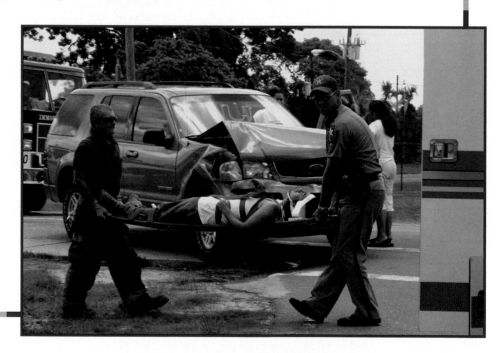

An **ambulance** takes an accident victim
directly to the emergency room.

Special Areas

Hospitals have many special areas. For example, the **maternity ward** is where women have babies. The **intensive care unit** is for patients with a serious condition.

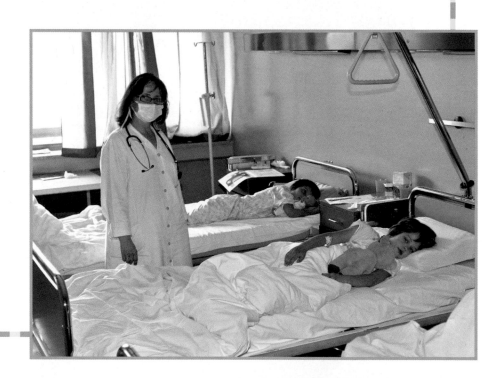

A newborn meets his brother and sisters for the first time.

A serious illness or injury may need surgery. That is what an operating room is for. Operating rooms are **sterile** rooms with

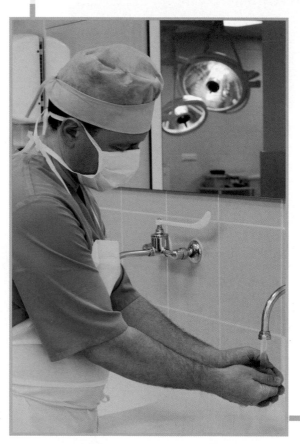

tools and machines that doctors and nurses use.

Doctors scrub their hands before surgery to wash away germs.

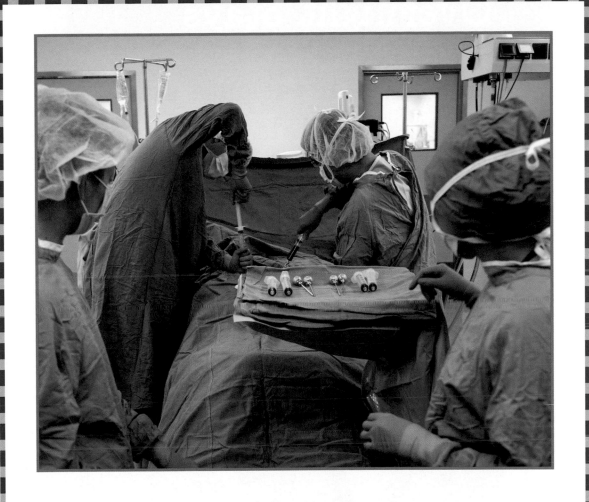

A team of doctors and nurses
operate on a patient.

Overnight Stays

Some hospital patients stay overnight. Hospitals have rooms with one bed, two beds, and rooms with many beds.

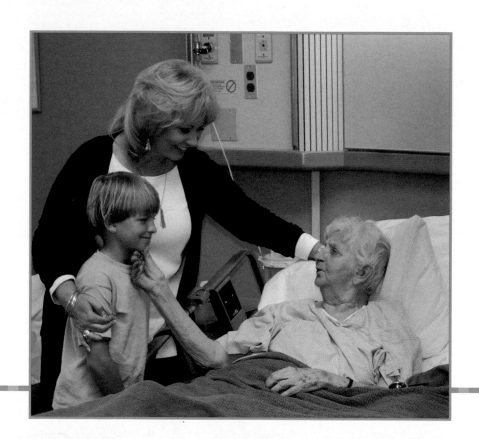

A favorite stuffed toy can make a hospital stay a little easier.

Visiting

Have you ever visited anyone in the hospital? Patients find it hard to be away from home. Visiting a friend or family member can help them feel better.

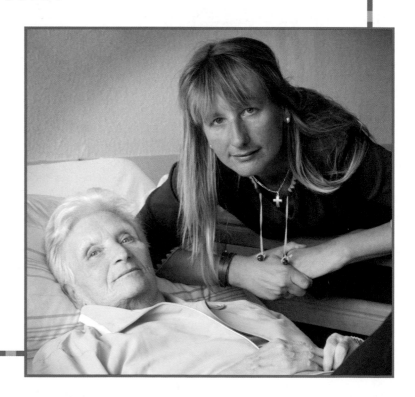

Putting a **SMILE**
on a patient's face
is **GOOD MEDICINE!**

Health Care
for the Community

Community hospitals have doctors and nurses who care for the health and well being of their patients.

Doctors and nurses help patients get the best medical care possible.

Glossary

ambulance (AM-byuh-luhns): a vehicle that takes sick or injured people to the hospital

expert (ek-SPURT): knowledgeable or skillful

intensive care unit (in-TENS-uhv-KAIR-YOO-nit): hospital area where close medical attention is given to patients with serious conditions

maternity ward (muh-TUR-nuh-tee-WORD): hospital area where women have babies

sterile (STER-uhl): free from germs

INDEX

FURTHER READING

Adamson, Heather. *A Day in the Life of a Doctor.* Capstone Press, 2004.

Gordon, Sharon. *What's Inside a Hospital?* Benchmark Books, 2006.

Kalman, Bobbie. *Hospital Workers in the Emergency Room.* Crabtree Publishing, 2004.

WEBSITES

www.hhs.gov/kids
www.bam.gov
bensguide.gpo.gov

ABOUT THE AUTHORS

David and Patricia Armentrout specialize in nonfiction children's books. They enjoy exploring different topics and have written about many subjects, including sports, animals, history, and people. David and Patricia love to spend their free time outdoors with their two boys and dog Max.